EATING VEGETARIAN

IN A NUTSHELL

EATING
VEGETARIAN
A STEP-BY-STEP
GUIDE

GAIL DUFF

ELEMENT

SHAFTESBURY, DORSET • BOSTON, MASSACHUSETTS • MELBOURNE, VICTORIA

© Element Books Limited 1999

First published in
Great Britain in 1999 by
ELEMENT BOOKS LIMITED
Shaftesbury, Dorset SP7 8BP

Published in the USA in 1999 by
ELEMENT BOOKS INC
160 North Washington Street, Boston
MA 02114

Published in Australia in 1999 by
ELEMENT BOOKS LIMITED
and distributed by Penguin Australia Ltd
487 Maroondah Highway, Ringwood,
Victoria 3134

NOTE FROM THE PUBLISHER
Unless specified otherwise
All recipes serve four
All eggs are medium
All herbs are fresh
All spoon measurements are level

Designed and created with
The Bridgewater Book Company Limited

ELEMENT BOOKS LIMITED
Managing Editor Miranda Spicer
Senior Commissioning Editor Caro Ness
Editor Finny Fox-Davies
Group Production Director Clare Armstrong
Production Manager Susan Sutterby
Production Controller Claire Legg

THE BRIDGEWATER
BOOK COMPANY
Art Director Terry Jeavons
Design and page layout Axis Design
Project Editor Caroline Earle
Editor Jo Wells
Photography David Jordan
Home Economy Judy Williams
Picture research Caroline Thomas

Printed and bound in Great Britain
by Butler & Tanner Ltd

Library of Congress Cataloging-in-
Publication data available

ISBN 1–86204–482–1

*The publishers wish to thank the following for
the use of pictures:* Tony Stone Images
pp.8BL, 8TR, 10, 11B, 14, 24, 28T
Mark Azavedo pp.9B
Garden Picture Library pp.26B

Contents

A way of life

EATING VEGETARIAN *is a whole new way of looking at the food on your plate and cooking vegetarian food is an adventure into new foods and cooking methods.*

Some vegetarian ingredients, such as eggs and dairy products, will already be familiar to you and are probably frequently used. Others, such as nuts and legumes, are well known, but how to turn them into balanced and enjoyable meals may be a mystery. Then there are ingredients such as bean curd and sesame paste which may only be unfamiliar ingredients on the shelf in the healthfood store. All of these foods can be used to make delicious main dishes.

If you decide to cut animal products out of your diet completely, even desserts may need to be rethought. You may need to look out for vegetarian substitutes. For example, you may wish to substitute a vegetarian setting agent, such as agar-agar, for gelatin in some recipes, such as mousses.

BEAN CURD

MEALS
When it comes to planning a vegetarian meal, ideas about vegetables simply being served as an accompaniment to a main meat dish will no longer be appropriate. Often, vegetarian meals are made by using a combination of

PASTA

ingredients to make one nutritious dish. More vegetables and carbohydrates (such as pasta or rice) will be used, than proteins.

RICE

Eating more vegetarian food and the changes this involves will add up to greater variety, improved flavor, enhanced appearance, and higher nutritional values.

DIFFERENT TYPES OF VEGETARIAN DIET

Lacto-vegetarians do not eat meat, poultry, game, or fish products, but will eat eggs and dairy foods, such as butter, cheese, and yogurt.

NUTS

By contrast, a vegan also cuts dairy products and eggs out of the diet. Nuts, legumes, and grains are an important source of protein in a vegan diet.

If you want to become a vegan, it is easier to begin gradually by continuing to eat dairy products for a while.

GRAINS

ABOVE **Chunky**
*vegetable soup makes
a healthy supper.*

BELOW **Apple mousse**
*made with agar-agar
instead of gelatin.*

Why be vegetarian?

PEOPLE DECIDE TO EAT VEGETARIAN *for a wide variety of reasons—to suit their budget, for better health, concern for animal welfare, ecological concern, or religious conviction. Some simply dislike the taste of meat, game, poultry, and fish and many people have discovered that vegetarian meals taste better and offer a greater variety than more conventional meat-based meals.*

Health is a significant reason for becoming vegetarian and it is not uncommon for people to feel healthier, fitter,

ABOVE *A vegetarian diet can help with weight loss.*

slimmer, and more "alive" when they change to a vegetarian diet. For example, by reducing your intake of animal products

LEFT *Many yoga practitioners prefer a vegetarian diet.*

STRAWBERRIES

and eating more fruit and vegetables in particular, you will increase the amount of fiber in your diet, which is good for the digestive system, keeps the bowels healthy, and can also reduce your calorie intake.

Some schools of thought even suggest

ASPARAGUS

BELOW *Vegetarianism is popular with those practicing alternative therapies, such as Reiki.*

that the human digestive system is simply not suitable for the healthy digestion of meat.

FOOD AND THE SPIRIT
Several religions, such as Hinduism and Buddhism, advocate a vegetarian diet and followers of many other religions believe that they are able to work within their faith more effectively if they exclude meat from their diet. The practitioners of alternative healing methods often share this point of view.

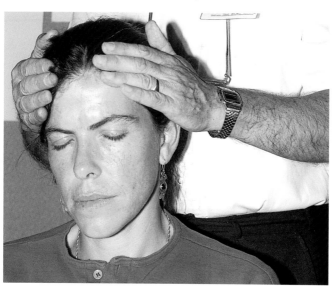

Vegetarian eating for health

MANY PEOPLE *have discovered that when they begin to eat a balanced vegetarian diet their health will improve quite noticeably and they rapidly feel fitter. There are also many long-term health benefits to eating a vegetarian diet.*

In the short term, a vegetarian diet can lead to a healthier digestive system, more energy, better hair and skin quality, and improved general health. In the long term, it can lower the risk of suffering from serious diseases, such as cancer, heart disease, diabetes, and bowel disorders.

ASSESSING YOUR DIET

One of the reasons for the short-term improvement in health is that a change in eating patterns often requires a detailed scrutiny of your diet in general. If you examine your daily or weekly intake of nutrients, this will probably highlight any problem areas or shortfalls which are then remedied.

Also, when you change your diet you will inevitably pay closer attention to the types of foods that you are buying.

LEFT **Regular exercise is just as important as a healthy diet.**

ABOVE *It is better to get vitamins from your diet, but supplements can also play a part in meeting your requirements.*

Gradually, processed and convenience foods will be left standing on the supermarket shelf in preference for fresh, natural, maybe even organic, ingredients. Vegetables will play a larger part in meal planning. More vegetables will be eaten at each meal, and there will be greater variety. This leads to a wider range of vitamins in every meal and an increased intake of fiber, which is good for the digestive system and general health.

RIGHT *Paying closer attention to the food you eat often leads to a healthier diet.*

The wholegrains and pastas that feature in vegetarian meals provide a constant source of energy that does not suffer the great swings, with high peaks and deep troughs, that refined flour and sugar products cause.

A LOW FAT DIET

A vegetarian diet will be lower in animal fats than a diet which includes meat, provided that high-fat dairy products are eaten in moderation only (especially cheese).

Meeting nutritional requirements

EATING A WELL-BALANCED *and varied diet will ensure that you get all the vitamins and minerals necessary for good health. However, it is important to maintain a balance of the right kind of protein when eating a wholly vegetarian diet.*

The human body needs protein to build muscles and repair tissues. However, it does not need a great deal and eating too much may even cause premature ageing. Men need an average of 2½–3 ounces protein per day and women 2–2½ ounces.

Traditionally, meat is the main source of protein in the diet. The main protein foods available to the vegetarian are eggs, dairy ingredients, legumes, nuts, and whole grain products, such as flour, rice, and pasta. There are also small amounts of protein in other foods,

WHOLE WHEAT FLOUR

EGGS

such as Brussels sprouts, green peas, and even dried apricots.

Proteins are made up of substances called amino acids. Protein foods have to contain the right combinations of these amino acids in order to be used by the body.

Eggs and dairy products are animal products and contain the right combinations of amino acids. Legumes, nuts, and whole grains all contain some of these amino acids in different combinations so, if eaten alone, they will not provide a "complete protein." However, if a balanced combination is eaten, the protein in a dish will be the same as that provided by meat.

Combining is easy. Think of beans on toast, whole wheat pasta coated in a nut sauce, or garbanzo bean curry with rice.

DRIED APRICOTS

COMPLETE PROTEIN FOODS

The exceptions to the rule that nuts, legumes, grains and vegetables provide partial amounts of essential proteins are soy beans and products

made from them, such as bean curd and soy milk, all of which are a "complete" protein.

Soy products are also an excellent source of vitamin B12, the only vitamin that may sometimes be lacking in a vegetarian diet. It is also found in eggs and dairy products.

LEFT *Combine beans with brown toast to provide the right amino acids.*

Vegetables

GREEN AND LEAFY, *round and red, sliced or chopped, steamed, boiled, or eaten raw, vegetables provide any number of culinary possibilities and a wide variety of vitamins and minerals. The fresher the vegetables, the better they are for you.*

At least two meals a day should be based on vegetables. Fresh vegetables are more nutritious than frozen or dried. Locally-grown organic vegetables are fresher than vegetables that have been imported and stored, so they have a higher nutritional value and do not contain any trace of chemical residues.

Store vegetables either in the refrigerator or in a cool, dry pantry, but eat them as soon after purchase as possible to maximize nutritional benefits.

ABOVE *Winter vegetable casseroles make warming main meals.*

SIDE DISHES

Vegetables used for side dishes can be steamed, lightly boiled, stir-fried, braised, or made into refreshing salads.

For main meals, vegetables can be made into casseroles, bakes, cobblers, pies, soups, spicy curries, toppings for pasta, vegetable molds and tasty omelets. Or stuff and bake individual vegetables, such as squash or eggplants.

LEFT *Market fresh vegetables are the most nutritious choice after growing your own.*

A QUICK GUIDE TO THE MAIN VITAMINS

Vitamin A: red- or orange-colored vegetables; green vegetables, such as broccoli, kale, spinach, and watercress

SPINACH

Vitamin B1 (thiamine): avocados, Jerusalem and globe artichokes, broccoli, Brussels sprouts, cauliflower, kale, mushrooms, parsnips, peas, potatoes, spinach, and watercress

CAULIFLOWER

Vitamin B2 (riboflavin): asparagus, frisée, runner beans, broccoli, cauliflower, peas, spinach

Vitamin B3 (niacin): mushrooms, asparagus, fava beans, parsnips, rutabagas, peas, potatoes

ASPARAGUS

Vitamin C: nearly all vegetables, highest in green types, such as bell peppers, broccoli, kale, Brussels sprouts, cabbage, and all varieties of cress and sprouted seeds

Vitamin K: all green vegetables

BELL PEPPER

PARSNIP

Fresh and dried fruit

FRUIT CAN BE INCORPORATED *in many ways into a vegetarian menu. As well as adding extra enjoyment, eating at least two different types of fruit every day can add significantly to the nutritional value and fiber content of the diet.*

There is nothing better than fresh fruit in season, bought in the best of condition and eaten as soon as possible.

Try chopped fresh fruit for breakfast with yogurt and muesli; have it as a snack in the morning or afternoon break, or as a quick dessert after lunch or dinner.

Fresh fruit can also be added to cooked side dishes and main dishes, as well as to savory salads in order to give a contrast in flavor and texture.

FRUIT JUICES
Fresh fruit juices are a versatile addition to savory dishes and salad dressings.

ABOVE *Orange juice makes a wonderful breakfast drink.*

ABOVE *Fuel your body for the day ahead with muesli, fruit and yogurt.*

A QUICK GUIDE TO THE MAIN VITAMINS

Vitamin A: all yellow- and orange-colored fresh fruit, such as apricots, mangoes, nectarines, peaches and yellow melons; dried apricots and peaches

APRICOTS

Vitamin B1 (thiamine): a little in most fresh fruits, particularly citrus fruits, pineapple, plums, melon, and bananas; currants, raisins, , prunes, and dried bananas

CURRANTS

Vitamin B2 (riboflavin): small amounts in most fresh and dried fruits

Vitamin B3 (niacin): small amounts in most fresh and dried fruits

Vitamin C: most fresh fruits. Those with the highest content are black currants, strawberries, citrus fruits, red currants, and gooseberries

Vitamin K: the pith of citrus fruit

LIME

BANANA

ORANGE AND LEMON SLICES

Cooked fresh fruit forms the basis of many desserts from warming pies and puddings to light, fluffy mousses.

Dried fruits are rich and sweet and bursting with goodness. They can help to cut down on added refined sugar in many sweet dishes or eaten sparingly as energy-giving snacks.

LEFT *Raisins are a high-energy snack, great for children at play. But they can be as bad for teeth as candies.*

Legumes

LEGUMES, OR PULSE VEGETABLES, *are the numerous dried beans, lentils, and peas. They are the valuable and versatile constituents of many vegetarian meals.*

An almost dizzying variety of beans is available in healthfood shops and supermarkets. The choice includes red, brown, and black kidney beans, black-eyed peas, speckled pinto beans, pale green small navy beans, creamy-colored garbanzo beans, KIDNEY BEANS and navy and lima beans, plus small, round, green mung beans, and red or adzuki beans. Soy beans are ivory colored, small and round.

Lentils also come in a wide variety of sizes and colors, each with GARBANZO BEANS

its own distinctive texture and flavor. There are split red lentils, whole green lentils, small brown lentils, and, in some Indian food stores, white lentils. LIMA BEANS Split yellow and green peas, the old-fashioned favorites, are also available.

Most legumes need to be soaked before they are cooked and they can have a long cooking time. Lentils, however, have the advantage SPLIT GREEN PEAS that they can be added directly to dishes, such as casseroles and soups, without having been soaked first and they cook relatively quickly.

1 To soak beans, put them into a saucepan of cold water and bring to a boil.

2 Boil rapidly for 10 minutes and then soak in the same water for at least 1 hour.

3 All beans vary but, after soaking, they will need to be simmered for at least 1 hour and maybe up to 2 hours. Using a pressure cooker will shorten the process considerably.

BEAN PRODUCTS

It is most convenient for quick meals to buy beans ready-cooked in cans.

There are also many products made from soy beans available. These include "soy grits," soy sausage mixes, and other meat substitutes, such as soy mince, soy milk, soy cream, and soy yogurts.

ABOVE *Soy milk can be used in place of cow's milk in some recipes.*

Bean curd, also known as tofu, is a form of soy bean "cheese" which can be served in a variety of ways.

A QUICK GUIDE TO THE MAIN VITAMINS

All beans and lentils contain the B group vitamins.

Soy beans and soy products also contain vitamin B12, which is especially valuable in a diet with few or no animal products.

SOY BEANS

Nuts and seeds

NUTS AND SEEDS *are small containers of concentrated goodness and they can be combined in modest amounts with other ingredients to make highly nutritious meals.*

Make sure that nuts and seeds are well within their "use-by" date when purchased and store them in a cool, dry pantry for no longer than one month. Nuts and seeds can become rancid and lose their nutritional value if they are stored for too long. Nuts are available both in the shell and shelled. Although they have a finer flavor if bought in the shell, a busy cook will save much time and trouble by buying them shelled. The exceptions are chestnuts and coconuts.

ABOVE **Nuts are fun to eat from the shell as a snack.**

If nuts are for chopping or grinding, it is often more economical to buy chopped nuts or "nut pieces" rather than nut halves, which are best kept for decoration.

ABOVE **Pumpkin seeds can add texture to recipes.**

Seeds, such as sunflower, pumpkin, and sesame seeds, all have similar nutritional values to nuts and can be used in many of the same ways.

Nuts and seeds can be used as ingredients in both savory and sweet dishes. Mix them into salads and

LEFT **Try scattering nuts or seeds onto a salad.**

ABOVE *Add nuts and seeds to muesli for extra protein.*

A QUICK GUIDE TO THE MAIN VITAMINS

B group vitamins: those highest in these vitamins are almonds, Brazil nuts, pine nuts, peanuts, and pistachios

ALMONDS

Vitamin C: cashew nuts

CASHEW NUTS

Vitamin D: sunflower seeds

Vitamin E: most nuts and seeds in varying amounts, particularly chestnuts and sunflower seeds

SUNFLOWER SEEDS

CHESTNUTS

cooked vegetables for side or main dishes, add them to stuffings and nut roasts; use them in bread doughs and cake mixtures, breakfast muesli and desserts.

Nut and seed products are also useful in the vegetarian kitchen. Peanut butter and sesame paste can be used as the base for salad dressings, dips, and sandwich fillings and can flavor cookies and baked goods.

Coconut milk, available canned, in cartons, and as a powder, is an authentic ingredient in Southeast Asian dishes. Cans of chestnut purée are convenient for both nut roasts and desserts.

LEFT *Garbanzo beans and Tahini makes a delicious creamy dip with crudités.*

Dairy products and eggs

MILK, CHEESE, YOGURT, CREAM, AND EGGS *are all part of a lacto-vegetarian diet. Use milk for sauces to top dishes such as lasagne or vegetable casseroles, or to make desserts. It is an essential ingredient in many bread and cake mixes.*

The type of milk you use, whether whole, skim, or low-fat, is a matter of personal preference. Goat's and sheep's milk can be used in the same way as cow's milk.

YOGURT

Yogurt is made by introducing a beneficial bacterium (*Lactobacillus acidophilus*) into milk.

ABOVE *Lasagne relies on cheese and milk for its creamy texture.*

The bacteria feed on the milk sugars and create a slight acidity. Yogurt is more easily digested than milk and it helps the body to digest other foods.

Yogurt can be used as a low-fat topping for both desserts and savory dishes, made into salad dressings and dips, stirred into soups and sauces, and whipped into mousses to give a creamy texture.

LEFT *Add yogurt to make a richer salad dressing.*

ABOVE **Strawberries and cream—the taste of summer.**

EGGS
One of the most versatile ingredients at the cook's disposal is eggs. They are an excellent source of protein.

CREAM
Although cream is high in fat, it need not be discarded altogether; there is nothing better on desserts. In cooking, substitute a low-fat creme fraiche or cream substitute.

LEFT **Use full flavoured hard cheeses sparingly.**

CHEESE
Flavorful cheeses make a versatile and useful ingredient when making vegetarian dishes, but try to choose reduced- or low-fat varieties. A small amount of grated, strongly flavored, hard cheese will go a long way to giving extra flavor to sauces, pasta dishes, nut roasts, and vegetable bakes. Soft cheese can be used for sauces and as a base for desserts, beaten into puréed vegetables instead of butter, or beaten with eggs as a tart filling.

A QUICK GUIDE TO THE MAIN VITAMINS

Vitamin A: eggs and cheese

B vitamins: eggs and cheese are good sources of vitamin B1 and vitamin B2, and also contain vitamin B12

Vitamin D: eggs and cheese

Vitamin E: small amount in eggs

EGGS

CHEESE

Grains and pasta

GRAINS AND PASTA *contain valuable carbohydrate for energy. Combined with legumes or nuts, they make a high-protein meal.*

G rains include wheat and wheat products, rice and the more unusual grains, such as maize, oats, rye, barley, millet, and buckwheat.

For the best nutritional value, choose whole grains or whole grain products.

All grains are made up of three parts. About 90 per cent of the grain is the white, starchy endosperm which provides

ABOVE *A loaf of bread begins here in a wheat field.*

carbohydrate. The outer husk, which provides the fiber, accounts for eight per cent, and two per cent consists of the germ that contains the protein and vitamins and minerals. Refined grain products, such as white flour or white rice, have the fiber and endosperm removed.

WHOLE WHEAT FLOUR

Therefore, they do not have as high a nutritional value as whole grain products.

ABOVE *Bulgar makes a filling salad.*

WHOLE WHEAT FLOUR

Whole wheat flour and pasta and brown rice are nutritionally important in a vegetarian diet, but it is not essential to use them all the time, especially if you feel that a dish would be better with one of the white varieties.

Use whole wheat flour for baking, whole wheat grains, or couscous as a side

BROWN RICE

dish and bulgar as a salad. Rice can be served boiled or fried, or made into a risotto, a paella, or a biriyani. Oatmeal is the base of muesli and flapjacks; barley makes a tasty addition to casseroles; and rye flour makes delicious bread. Both millet and buckwheat make unusual side dishes.

ABOVE *Couscous can be served as a side dish.*

A QUICK GUIDE TO THE MAIN VITAMINS

B vitamins: a selection are in all whole grains in varying proportions. Oats contain more Vitamin B1 than any other grain

Vitamin E: wheat

Vegetarian storecupboard

A NUMBER OF EXTRA INGREDIENTS *help to make the basic vegetarian ingredients into exciting main meals.*

Herbs and spices are essential to any cook. Herbs can be grown at home or bought fresh or dried. Most are easy to grow in a small patch in the garden, in tubs, window-boxes, or even in flower pots. The perennial herbs, thyme, marjoram, savory, and sage, will last for many years once they have become established. Annuals, such as basil and dill, and biennial parsley should be sown each year in the spring. But if you have neither the space nor the time to do this, it is now easy to

BASIL

PARSLEY

BELOW *A herb garden looks beautiful and brings the taste of the garden into the kitchen*

ABOVE **You can grow your own cilantro on a windowsill.**

flavor will begin to diminish. Spices, too, should not be kept for any more than six months. Store them in a dark, dry place. Vegetable

DRIED HERBS

stock can be made by boiling chopped vegetables in water to which 2 tablespoons of soy or tamari sauce can be added to give extra flavor. Mild tasting vegetable bouillon cubes that do not contain monosodium glutamate can also be used.

cheat. Supermarkets, other stores, and markets sell growing herbs in plastic pots which are perfect for the busy cook who wants to use fresh herbs but does not have a homegrown supply.

Buy dried herbs in small amounts and do not keep them for longer than six months. After this, the aroma and

RIGHT **Herbs are an essential in any kitchen.**

For setting desserts, the most widely used vegetarian substitute for gelatin is agar-agar, which is made from seaweed and comes in the form of colorless crystals. The amount needed will vary from brand to brand, so it is always best to consult the manufacturer's instructions on the packet.

Planning daily menus

FOOD NEEDS TO BE ENJOYED, *it has to be interesting, and should contain a wide range of vitamins and minerals. It therefore pays to spend a little thought on the meals that you will cook and eat during the day to ensure that there is plenty of variety in the ingredients and cooking and serving methods.*

ABOVE **Meal times are an important part of family life.**

BREAKFAST

- A whole grain cereal or muesli with low sugar content, plus yogurt or milk, and a piece of fresh fruit.
- Chopped fresh fruit with a handful of muesli topped with yogurt.

PIECE OF APPLE

- Porridge topped with honey, plus a piece of fresh fruit.
- Two slices of whole wheat toast spread with butter or low-fat spread and honey or yeast extract, plus fresh fruit or a broiled tomato.
- One poached or boiled egg with one slice whole wheat bread or toast.

LIGHT MEAL

- Salad with a small amount of protein, such as cheese or nuts, plus one or two slices of whole wheat bread.
- A potato baked in its jacket served with a small portion of green or mixed salad.
- Thick vegetable soup with slices of whole wheat bread and fresh fruit.
- Vegetarian pizza served with a salad or fresh fruit.

ABOVE *Quiche can be served hot or cold.*

BELOW *A simple lunch of baked potato and salad.*

MAIN MEAL

- Cooked dish of vegetables and legumes with a whole grain accompaniment, such as brown rice or couscous.
- Quiche or other egg dish with a salad or a selection of cooked vegetables and a jacket potato.
- Nut dish with a salad or a selection of cooked vegetables.
- Stir-fried vegetable dish with bean curd or nuts, accompanied by brown rice.
- Whole wheat pasta with a cheese or nut coating, topped with a vegetable sauce or mixed vegetables.

Utensils

THE UTENSILS *that are used for vegetarian cooking can be found in most well-equipped kitchens. Good quality sharp knives are essential for preparing and chopping vegetables. With the right selection of knives, you should be able to dispense with kitchen gadgets such as herb choppers and garlic crushers.*

A large, heavy, good quality vegetable knife is invaluable for dicing root vegetables, shredding cabbage, and chopping onions and herbs. Smaller, pointed knives are useful for coring and seeding bell peppers and chilies. Small serrated knives are best for fruit and soft vegetables, such as tomatoes. Match knives with a heavy chopping board and they should last for many years.

A vegetable steamer is a great asset in the vegetarian kitchen. The best are about 8–10 inches in diameter and can fit easily into their own

BELOW *You will need knives in a variety of sizes.*

CHOPPING BOARD

saucepan; 1 pound or more vegetables can then be steamed at a time, either loose inside the

CHOPPING VEGETABLES

DICING VEGETABLES

SHREDDING VEGETABLES

steamer or in foil-wrapped packets. Dishes of sweet custard and savory egg mixtures can also be fitted inside a vegetable steamer.

SAUCEPANS

The best saucepans to use are cast iron or stainless steel with well-fitting lids. A selection of casseroles is also very useful. Equipment for puréeing soups and sauces can save time and effort, but if time is not important, a hand vegetable mill makes delicious textured

ABOVE *Hand blenders are useful for puréeing small quantities.*

soups. An electric hand blender, a small blender or a food processor can be used.

LEFT *For creating smooth soups and pasta sauces a food processor is invaluable.*

Thick Vegetable Soup

THIS IS A SIMPLY-MADE, *but wholesome, warming, and flavorsome soup suitable for lunch or supper at any time of the year.*

INGREDIENTS

2½ cups vegetable stock

8 ounces celery stalks, finely chopped

8 ounces carrots, finely chopped

8 ounces tomatoes, skinned, chopped

8 ounces potatoes, chopped

1 large onion, finely chopped

bouquet garni

salt and freshly ground black pepper

⅔ cup plain yogurt

1 garlic clove, crushed

watercress leaves, to garnish

**Serves 4 as a starter,
2 as a light meal**

VARIATION

● All the vegetables may be blended together before adding to the pan in order to make a smoother soup.

● Chopped parsley or chervil may be used instead of watercress.

WATERCRESS

1 Bring the vegetable stock to a boil in a large saucepan. Add the chopped vegetables and bouquet garni. Season lightly. Cover and simmer for 20 minutes.

2 Discard the bouquet garni.
Puree all the liquid and
three-quarters of the vegetables
in a blender or food processor.

3 Add the yogurt and
garlic and process again.
Stir the soup back into the
saucepan with the remaining
vegetables. Reheat gently,
without boiling. Serve in
individual bowls garnished
with watercress and freshly
ground black pepper.

COOK'S TIP

To skin the tomatoes, put
them into a bowl and pour
over boiling water. Leave for
30–60 seconds, depending
on their firmness. The skins
should then slip off easily.

Hummus with Toasted Sesame Seeds

PARSLEY AND SESAME SEEDS *add color and flavor to a garbanzo bean dip. Serve as a starter or as part of a buffet or picnic.*

INGREDIENTS

8 ounces cooked or canned garbanzo beans

2 tablespoons sesame seeds

1 garlic clove, crushed

juice of 1 lemon

2 tablespoons sesame paste

4 tablespoons olive oil

½ cup chopped parsley

pinch of chili powder

FOR THE GARNISH

2 black olives, halved

12 ounces tomatoes, sliced

2 small onions, sliced into rings

4 parsley sprigs

ONION RINGS

1 Pass the garbanzo beans through the fine blade of a vegetable mill or purée in a blender or food processor. Transfer to a bowl.

COOK'S TIP

To cook dried garbanzo beans, bring to a boil in a saucepan and boil rapidly for 10 minutes. Remove the pan from the heat and leave the beans for 2 hours. Return to a boil, cover, and simmer for 1½ hours, or until are soft. Drain.

2 Reserve 4 teaspoons of the sesame seeds and stir the rest in a dry, heavy skillet over medium heat for about 2 minutes, or until evenly browned. Tip immediately onto a plate to cool.

3 Beat the sesame seeds, garlic, lemon juice, and sesame paste into the bean purée, then beat in the oil, a teaspoonful at a time. Stir in the parsley and chili powder.

4 Put a portion of the hummus into the center of each of 4 small plates. Arrange the tomatoes and onions around the hummus. Serve with warm pita bread. Top each portion with a sprinkling of sesame seeds, half an olive, and a sprig of parsley.

Root Vegetable Mold

EGGS AND CHEESE *turn grated root vegetables into a light—textured mold for a main course.*

INGREDIENTS

1⅓ cups grated carrots

1 cup grated rutabaga

2 parsnips, grated

freshly ground black pepper

2 sage leaves

3 sprigs of thyme

3 eggs, beaten

1 cup grated Cheddar cheese

1 tablespoon tomato paste

⅛ nutmeg, freshly grated

1 pound broccoli flowerets, freshly steamed

FOR THE SAUCE

14 ounce can chopped tomatoes

2 tablespoons butter, plus extra for greasing

2 tablespoons whole wheat flour

1 Mix the grated vegetables together and put in a steamer. Season with pepper. Add the sage and 2 thyme sprigs, then cover, and steam for 15 minutes, or until just tender. Discard the herbs and leave the vegetables to cool.

2 Beat the eggs with the cheese, tomato paste, and nutmeg.

BROCCOLI

3 Mix in the root vegetables. Fill a greased 8-inch ring mold with the egg and vegetable mixture. Cover with foil. Place in a roasting pan with water to come halfway up the sides. Cook in a preheated oven at 350°F for 45 minutes, or until set.

4 To make the sauce, bring the tomatoes, butter, flour, and the remaining thyme to a boil, stirring constantly, until the mixture has thickened. Remove the thyme.

5 Turn the mould on to a plate and fill the center with the broccoli. Serve the sauce separately.

THYME

Pasta with Walnut Pesto

THIS FILLING PASTA *is served with a warm avocado and tomato salad that adds contrasting flavor and color.*

INGREDIENTS

FOR THE PESTO

1 cup shelled walnuts

3 garlic cloves, chopped

6 tablespoons chopped basil

⅔ cup freshly grated Parmesan cheese

½ cup olive oil

2 tablespoons unsalted butter, softened

salt and freshly ground black pepper

12 ounces fresh tagliatelle

FOR THE SALAD

2 ripe avocados, peeled and cut in
½-inch cubes

4 tablespoons olive oil

2 tablespoons white wine vinegar

1 pound small, vine-ripened tomatoes,
skinned, halved, and seeded

freshly ground black pepper

GARLIC
CLOVES

1 To make the pesto, mix all the ingredients to a smooth paste in a small food processor or blender.

2 Cook the tagliatelle in salted boiling water until just tender. Drain well, then return to the pan, and set it over very low heat. Fold in the pesto and take the pan from the heat.

3 Put the avocado and tomatoes in a small saucepan with the oil, vinegar, and black pepper. Place over low heat and turn the contents gently until just warmed through. Do not allow to overheat or boil.

4 Divide the pasta among 4 serving plates and spoon the salad over the top.

AVOCADO

Deep-fried Bean Curd with Peanut Salad

HOT, DEEP-FRIED BEAN CURD, *meltingly soft on the inside, contrasts with the crunchy vegetables in this Chinese-inspired dish.*

INGREDIENTS

FOR THE SALAD DRESSING

4 tablespoons sesame oil or olive oil

juice of ½ lemon

1 teaspoon honey

½ teaspoon ground ginger

1 garlic clove, crushed

FOR THE TOFU DRESSING

2 tablespoons sesame paste

1 tablespoon soy sauce

1 tablespoon white wine vinegar

1 tablespoon rice wine or sherry (optional)

1 teaspoon chili sauce or Tabasco sauce

1 garlic clove, crushed

1 tablespoon cold water

FOR THE SALAD

½ cucumber, cut in ½-inch cubes

½ cup salted peanuts

1 pound firm bean curd, cut in ½-inch cubes

vegetable oil for deep-frying

½ Chinese cabbage, shredded

1 green bell pepper, cored, seeded. and thinly sliced lengthwise

½ cup bean sprouts

VARIATION

If Chinese cabbage is not available use an Iceberg lettuce.

1 To make the salad dressing beat all the ingredients together in a large bowl.

2 To make the bean curd dressing, gradually beat the remaining ingredients into the sesame paste to give a mayonnaise-like consistency.

3 Put the cucumber into a large bowl together with the peanuts.

4 Fill a pan with vegetable oil to a depth of about 4 inches and heat to 350°F. Fry the bean curd cubes a few at a time until crisp and golden. Drain quickly and add to the cucumber and peanuts. Fold in the bean curd dressing.

5 Fold the salad dressing into the Chinese cabbage, bell pepper, and bean sprouts. Arrange the salad on a large, flat, serving plate. Spoon the bean curd over the salad.

Middle Eastern Tagine with Couscous

COUSCOUS, *a form of cracked wheat, is popular in Morocco, Tunisia, and Algeria. It goes really well with spiced Middle Eastern style stews.*

EGGPLANT

INGREDIENTS

1 eggplant, about 12 ounces, cut into ½-inch thick pieces

salt

1 onion, thinly sliced

2 garlic cloves, chopped

4 tablespoons olive oil

1 each red and green bell pepper, thinly sliced lengthwise

½ cauliflower, divided into flowerets

2 fresh red or green chilies, seeded and finely chopped

1 teaspoon ground turmeric

14 ounces cooked or canned garbanzo beans, drained

14 ounces cooked or canned green lentils, drained

1¼ cups vegetable stock

2 tablespoons tomato paste

1⅓ cups couscous

1¼ cups boiling water

½ cup slivered almonds

2 tablespoons butter

4 tablespoons chopped cilantro

COOK'S TIP

Some types of couscous may vary in the manufacturer's recommended cooking method. If in doubt, follow the instructions on the packet.

CAULIFLOWER FLOWERETS

1 Put the eggplant into a
colander, sprinkle with salt
and leave for 30 minutes. Rinse
under running cold water and
dry with paper towels.

2 Gently cook the onion and
garlic in the oil in a large
skillet for about 2 minutes, or
until transparent.

3 Add the remaining
vegetables and fry for
4 minutes. Stir in the turmeric,
garbanzo beans, lentils, and
stock and bring to a boil.

4 Add the tomato paste,
cover, and leave to simmer
for 30 minutes.

5 Soak the couscous in the
boiling water until all the
water has been absorbed and
the couscous is soft.

6 Brown the almonds in the
butter. Mix in the couscous,
with a fork so the grains stay
separate. Fork in the cilantro.
Pile around the edge of a large,
flat plate. Spoon the vegetables
into the center.

Leek and Camembert Omelet

OMELETS *always make tasty, easily prepared suppers. This one has sliced Camembert cheese melting into the top.*

INGREDIENTS

1 cup thinly sliced leeks

2 tablespoons butter

6 eggs

2 teaspoons chopped tarragon

4 tablespoons chopped chervil or parsley

pepper

4 ounces Camembert cheese, thinly sliced

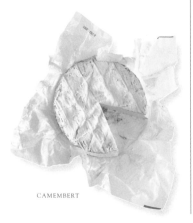

CAMEMBERT

1 Gently cook the leek in the butter in a large skillet until softened.

2 Beat the eggs with the herbs and pepper. Stir into the pan.

VARIATION

Brie can be used instead of Camembert.

3 Cook the omelet, lifting the sides as they set and tipping the skillet to let as much of the liquid as possible flow down to the base.

4 When the underneath is set and the omelet is about half cooked through, arrange the sliced Camembert on top.

5 Put the omelette under a hot broiler until the top sets and rises, and browns around the cheese.

6 Serve cut into wedges with a lightly dressed salad.

Carrots, Leeks, and Mustard

THIS COLORFUL COMBINATION *of carrots and leeks makes a tasty side dish to accompany hot main courses.*

INGREDIENTS

4–6 medium carrots, cut in thin strips

3 cups sliced leeks

2 tablespoons butter or sunflower oil

scant 1 cup vegetable stock

2 teaspoons mild whole grain mustard

COOK'S TIP

If using a bouillon cube, choose a make that has a mild flavor and a low salt content. Make up the bouillon cube with boiling water before adding to the dish.

1 Cook the sliced carrots and leeks in the butter or oil in a saucepan over high heat for 1 minute.

2 Pour in the stock and bring to a boil.

3 Gently fold in the mustard. Cover and cook over medium heat for 15 minutes, or until the carrots are just tender and most of the stock has evaporated.

VARIATION

Instead of mustard, fresh herbs may be used, such as 2 tablespoons chopped chervil, 4 tablespoons chopped parsley or 1 tablespoon mixed chopped thyme and marjoram.

LEEKS

Braised Fennel with Orange

THE COLOR AND TASTE *of the orange contrasts with the fennel, and the fruit gives this dish a refreshing flavor.*

INGREDIENTS

2 large oranges

2 large fennel bulbs, thinly sliced, (fennel leaves, chopped)

2 tablespoons butter

4 tablespoons vegetable stock

1 Grate the rind and squeeze the juice from 1 orange.

2 Melt the butter in a flameproof casserole on medium heat. Put the fennel, stock, orange rind, orange juice, and chopped fennel leaves into the casserole dish and bring to a boil.

3 Cover the casserole and cook in a preheated oven at 350°F for 45 minutes.

ORANGES

4 Cut the peel and pith from the remaining orange. Cut the flesh into fourths and slice them thinly.

5 Add the orange pieces to the casserole. Return the casserole to the oven for 2 minutes to warm through.

VARIATION

Scatter 1 tablespoon freshly grated Parmesan cheese into the dish after adding the pieces of orange.

Rice with Peas and Cashew Nuts

CRUNCHY CASHEW NUTS *and succulent green peas add protein and texture to rice, while turmeric colors it yellow.*

INGREDIENTS

1 small onion, finely chopped

½ cup butter or olive or sunflower oil

1½ cups long grain brown rice

2 teaspoons ground turmeric

3 cups vegetable stock

salt

2 cups shelled peas (fresh or frozen)

½ cup cashew nuts

4 tablespoons chopped parsley

1 Soften the onion in half the butter or oil in a saucepan over low heat.

2 Stir in the rice and turmeric, then add the stock, and bring to a boil.

CASHEW NUTS

PEAS

VARIATION

Slivered almonds can be used instead of cashew nuts.

3 Season with salt. Cover and simmer for 25 minutes.

4 Add the peas and continue to cook until all the stock has been absorbed.

5 Meanwhile, fry the cashew nuts in the remaining butter or oil over medium heat, stirring constantly, until they are golden.

6 As soon as the rice is cooked, fork in the cashew nuts and parsley.

Bell Pepper and Frisée Salad

PAPRIKA

SALADS *always make a refreshing accompaniment to cooked meals. The bright greens and reds of this nutritious salad make it an attractive addition to any table.*

INGREDIENTS

FOR THE DRESSING

4 tablespoons olive oil

2 tablespoons cider vinegar

1 garlic clove, crushed with a pinch of sea salt

1 tablespoon tomato paste

1 teaspoon paprika

1 teaspoon Tabasco sauce

FOR THE SALAD

4 ounces mixed salad and frisée leaves

1 large red bell pepper, cored, seeded, and cut in 1-inch strips

2 tablespoons currants

1 To make the dressing, put the olive oil into a salad bowl. Add the vinegar and then beat in the remaining ingredients.

FRISÉE LEAVES

COOK'S TIP

To crush the garlic without a garlic crusher, finely chop it, leave it on the chopping board, and sprinkle it with a pinch of sea salt. Use the tip of a small, round-bladed, flexible knife to crush it.

2 Toss the salad leaves and bell pepper in the dressing.

3 Scatter the currants over the top.

VARIATION

● Use only frisée if a more bitter flavor is preferred.

● Batavia may be used if the frisée is not available.

● Extra currants may be added to taste.

Apple Mousse

THIS LUXURIOUS DESSERT *uses soft, silken bean curd instead of cream, and agar-agar as a replacement for gelatin. Together they give the mousse a light, fluffy consistency.*

INGREDIENTS

FOR THE MOUSSE

1 pound cooking apples,
cored and chopped

⅔ cup natural apple juice

¼ cup honey

agar-agar or proprietary vegetarian
setting agent to set 2½ cups liquid
(see manufacturer's instructions)

2 eggs, separated

10 ounces silken tofu, rubbed
through a strainer

FOR THE DECORATION

2 eating apples, quartered and sliced

⅔ cup natural apple juice

¼ cup honey

3 tablespoons chopped toasted hazelnuts
or 1 tsp cinnamon

CHOPPED
HAZELNUTS

1 Gently cook the apples in a covered saucepan with 4 tablespoons apple juice for 15 minutes, or until soft.

2 Rub the apples and juice through a strainer.

3 Dissolve the setting agent in remaining apple juice.

4 Return the apple purée to the saucepan. Mix in the honey and the apple juice. Bring to just below boiling over medium heat.

5 Off the heat, beat in the egg yolks, one at a time. Leave to cool until just warm, but not set.

6 Whisk the egg whites until stiff. Fold the bean curd and then the egg whites into the apple mixture. Divide between 4 individual dessert dishes and leave in a cool place for 2 hours to set.

7 To make the decoration, bring the apple juice and honey to a boil. Put in the apple slices and cook them gently until transparent, but not too soft. Lift the apples onto a plate to cool.

8 Decorate the desserts with the apple slices and cinnamon or nuts just before serving.

Orange and Marmalade Cake

BECAUSE IT IS MADE WITH CORN OIL *instead of butter, this cake has a light, sponge texture.*

MARMALADE

INGREDIENTS

FOR THE CAKE

1½ cups whole wheat flour

salt

1 teaspoon baking powder

½ cup light muscovado sugar

grated rind and juice of 1 large orange

2 tablespoons no-sugar-added marmalade

½ cup corn oil, plus extra for greasing

2 eggs, separated

FOR THE FILLING AND DECORATION

½ cup cream cheese

3 tablespoons no-sugar-added marmalade

¼ cup chopped, toasted hazelnuts

Makes one 7-inch sandwich cake

1 Lightly oil two 7-inch cake pans.

2 Mix the flour with the salt, baking powder, sugar, and orange rind. Make a well in the center of the mixture.

MUSCOVADO SUGAR

3 Make up the orange juice to 5 tablespoons with cold water, if necessary, then pour into the well with the marmalade, corn oil, and egg yolks.

4 Beat with a wooden spoon to a fairly stiff mixture.

5 Whisk the egg whites until stiff and gently fold into the cake mixture.

6 Divide between the cake pans. Bake in a preheated oven at 350°F for 20 minutes, or until firm and slightly shrunk from the sides of the pan. Turn the cakes onto wire racks to cool.

VARIATION

- Grate a little orange rind over the top.
- Scatter 2 tablespoons ground almonds over the top.

7 To make the filling, beat the marmalade into the cream cheese. Use the mixture to sandwich the cakes together and to decorate. Sprinkle the top with chopped hazelnuts.

Further reading

VEGETARIAN COOKBOOK, *Gail Duff's*
(Macmillan London Ltd, 1978)

VEGETARIAN FOOD FOR FRIENDS,
Lyn Weller (HarperCollins, 1998)

BROADER THAN BEANS, *Lesley Waters*
(Headline, 1998)

LINDA'S KITCHEN, *Linda McCartney*
(Little Brown, 1995)

LINDA MCCARTNEY ON TOUR –
OVER 200 MEAT-FREE DISHES
FROM AROUND THE WORLD
(Little Brown, 1998)

GOOD HOUSEKEEPING STEP-BY-STEP
VEGETARIAN COOKBOOK
(Ebury, 1997)

THE NEW VEGETARIAN COOKBOOK,
Heather Thomas (HarperCollins, 1998)

Useful addresses

The Vegetarian Society
Parkdale
Durham Rd
Altrincham
Cheshire WA14 4QG
England

**The Vegetarian Union of
North America**
PO Box 9710
Washington DC20016
USA

**The Australian
Vegetarian Society**
PO Box 65
2021 Paddington
Australia

The Soil Association
86 Colston St
Bristol BS! 5BB
England

Farm Verified Organic
RR 1
Box 40A USA
Medina
ND 58467
USA

**National Association for
Sustainable Agriculture**
PO Box 768
AUS-Sterling
SA5152
Australia

Other Books in the Series

&